I WONDER Why

Camels Have Humps

and other questions about animals

Anita Ganeri

KINGFISHER

NEW YORK

Copyright © Kingfisher 2012
Published in the United States by Kingfisher,
175 Fifth Ave., New York, NY 10010
Kingfisher is an imprint of Macmillan Children's Books,
London.
All rights reserved.

First published 1993 by Kingfisher
This edition published 2012 by Kingfisher

Consultant: Michael Chinery

Distributed in the U.S. and Canada by Macmillan,
175 Fifth Ave., New York, NY 10010

Library of Congress Cataloging-in-Publication data
has been applied for.

ISBN: 978-0-7534-6702-2 (HC)
ISBN 978-0-7534-6701-5 (PB)

Kingfisher books are available for special promotions and
premiums. For details contact: Special Markets Department,
Macmillan, 175 Fifth Ave., New York, NY 10010.

For more information, please visit www.kingfisherbooks.com

Printed in China
9 8 7 6 5 4 3 2 1
1TR/1011/WKT/UNTD/140MA

Illustrations: Stephen Holmes (Eunice McMullen);
Tony Kenyon (B.L. Kearley) all cartoons.

CONTENTS

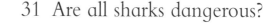

Female Queen Alexandra's birdwings are the world's biggest butterflies. Their wings are as big as this page!

The blue whale is so long that eight elephants could stand along its back.

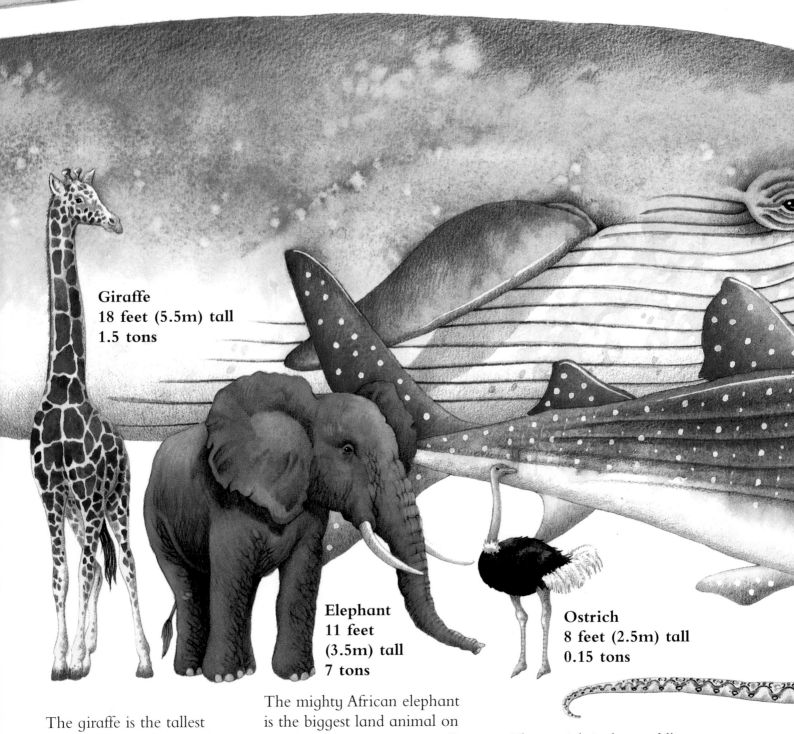

Giraffe
18 feet (5.5m) tall
1.5 tons

Elephant
11 feet (3.5m) tall
7 tons

Ostrich
8 feet (2.5m) tall
0.15 tons

The giraffe is the tallest land animal. With its long neck, it can reach as high as a two-story house.

The mighty African elephant is the biggest land animal on Earth. It is three times as tall as you are and can weigh as much as seven cars.

The ostrich is the world's tallest and heaviest bird. It's as tall as a bus!

Which is the biggest animal?

The biggest animal that has ever lived is the blue whale—it is even larger than the biggest dinosaurs were. Blue whales can weigh as much as 150 cars!

The whale shark weighs as much as 40 cars. It's the world's biggest fish.

Blue whale
100 ft. (30m) long
150 tons

Person
5–6 feet
(1.6–1.9m) tall

Whale shark
50 feet (15m) long
40 tons

The reticulated python can grow to be as long as a row of six bicycles! It's the world's longest snake.

Reticulated python 33 feet (10m) long

What's the difference between sharks and dolphins?

Although sharks and dolphins look alike, they belong to two very different animal groups. A shark is a kind of fish, but dolphins are members of another group—mammals.

You don't look anything like a dolphin, but you are a mammal, too!

If an animal breathes air into its lungs and its babies feed on their mother's milk, it's a mammal. Most mammals have some fur or hair on their bodies.

Lungs

If an animal has feathers and hatches out of a hard-shelled egg, it's a bird. All birds have wings, and most of them can fly.

If an animal has six legs and three parts to its body, it's an insect. There are more kinds of insects in the world than all of the other kinds of animals put together.

Abdomen

Head / **Thorax**

If an animal has damp, slimy skin and is born in water but lives much of its life on land, it's an amphibian. Baby amphibians hatch out of jellylike eggs.

If an animal has dry, scaly skin and is born on land, it's a reptile. Most reptiles lay eggs with leathery skin.

Scaly skin ———— **Fin**

Gills

If an animal lives in water, breathing through gills and using fins to move, it's a fish. Most fish lay jellylike eggs that hatch into baby fish.

7

What's the difference between . . . frogs and toads?

Frogs usually have smooth skin and long legs for leaping. Most toads have bumpy skin and move their short, thick bodies around by crawling.

Toad

Frog

Frogs and toads are both amphibians.

. . . and alligators and crocodiles?

Crocodiles have longer, more pointed snouts than alligators. A crocodile also has one very large tooth sticking up on each side when it closes its mouth.

Alligators and crocodiles are both reptiles.

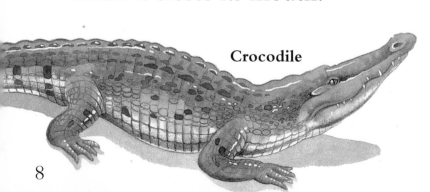

Crocodile

Alligator

. . . and monkeys and apes?

The big difference between these animals is that monkeys have long tails, but apes don't have tails at all. There are many different kinds of monkeys, but the only apes are gorillas, orangutans, chimpanzees, gibbons, and humans.

Spider monkey

Monkeys and apes are mammals.

(ap

A pill bug looks like an insect, but it isn't— it has too many legs! This creepy-crawly is related to crabs and lobsters.

. . . and rabbits and hares?

Hares have longer legs and ears than rabbits. Their whiskers are longer, too.

Rabbits and hares are both mammals.

Rabbit   **Hare**

o animals have ns inside their bodies?

imals have skeletons, but
e ones do. This is because
r an animal is, the more it
ng, sturdy framework to
ogether and carry its
tons also protect soft
, such as brains and hearts.

s with backbones
lled vertebrates. Fish
rtebrates, and so are
phibians, reptiles, birds,
nd mammals.

Backbone

Backbone

Animals without backbones
are called invertebrates.
Insects, spiders, snails, worms,
jellyfish, shrimps, and crabs
are all invertebrates.

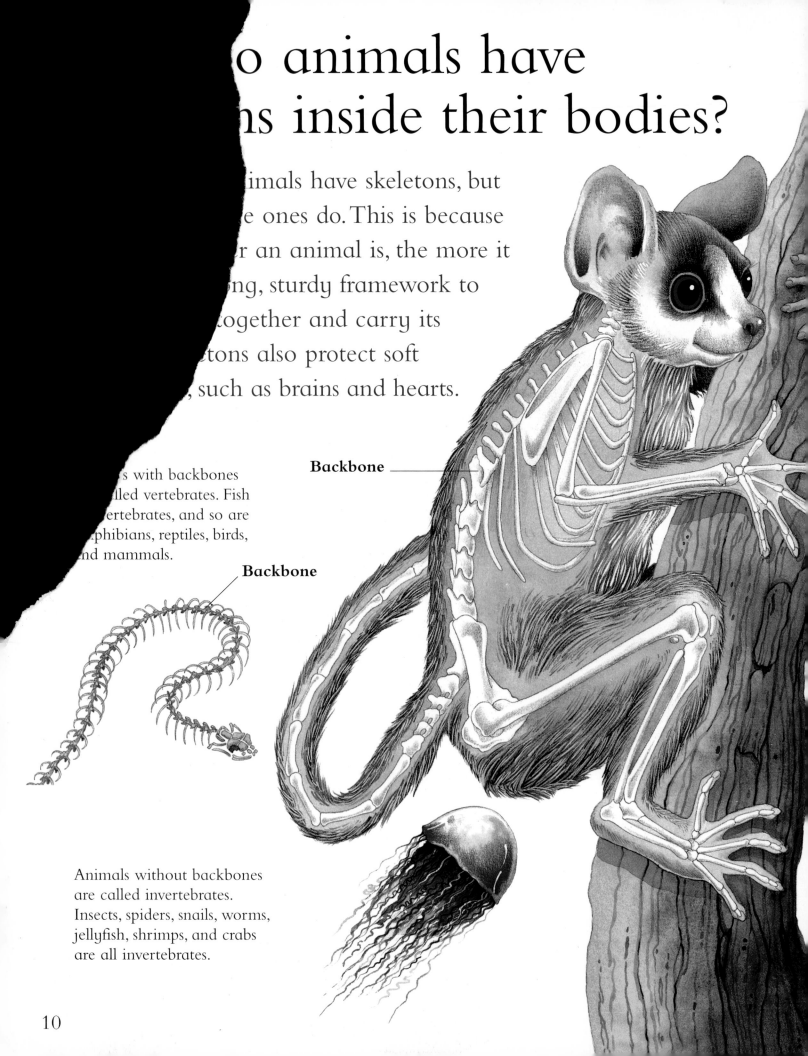

Most animals' skeletons are made of bone, but a shark's skeleton is made of gristle. This isn't as hard as bone, but it's still tough. You have some on the tip of your nose.

Insects, spiders, scorpions, centipedes, and millipedes all have tough exoskeletons.

Lobsters, crabs, and some beetles have very tough exoskeletons that work like armor to protect them from attacks.

Why d
skeleton

Not all an
most larg
the bigge
needs a stro
hold its body
weight. Skele
inside parts

o
m
fro

Animal
are cova
are vs!
am
a

Which animals have skeletons on the outside?

Most smaller animals have tough skins called exoskeletons. These outside skeletons do the same job as inside ones. They protect and support animals' soft bodies.

To grow larger, an animal has to break out of its old exoskeleton and grow a new one.

Why do camels have humps?

A camel's hump is its own built-in food cupboard. By living off the fat stored in its hump, a camel can go for as long as two weeks without eating. Camels need their humps because they live in deserts, where food and water are hard to find.

Why do elephants have trunks?

An elephant's trunk is a helpful tool. It can be used to pull down leaves and branches to eat. It also makes a good hose—elephants can squirt dust or water over themselves to stay cool.

Elephants say "hello" to friends by shaking trunks with them.

An elephant's trunk is a little like a hand. Using its tip, an elephant can pick up something as small as a button.

An Arabian camel has one hump.

A Bactrian camel has two humps.

A thirsty camel can drink ten buckets of water in only ten minutes!

Why do giraffes have long necks?

A giraffe's long neck makes it tall enough to eat the leaves at the tops of trees. Other animals cannot reach as high, so the giraffe has lots to eat.

A giraffe's tongue is 20 inches (0.5m) long!

13

Which bird has eyes in the back of its head?

An owl's eyes aren't really in the back of its head, but at times they might as well be! Owls have such flexible necks that when they want to look backward, they just swivel their heads around!

An owl's huge eyes help it see at night. This is when most owls fly around hunting for food.

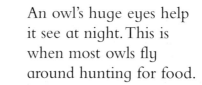

How do bats see in the dark?

Bats not only speed around at night without bumping into things, but they also manage to hunt down juicy insects to eat. Bats can do this even when it's pitch-black, because they use sound, not light, to find their way.

Bats make lots of very high squeaking sounds as they fly. When these sounds hit objects—such as insects or trees—they bounce off them, back toward the bats. The repeated sounds are called echoes. Bats can tell where things are by listening to the echoes.

The blue-tongued skink sticks out its big blue tongue to frighten enemies away.

Starfish don't have heads, but they do have eyes. They are on the ends of their arms.

Which animals smell with their tongues?

Snakes and lizards don't smell with their noses like we do. Instead, they flick their long tongues in and out. Their tongues pick up smells from the air and the ground, helping them track down things to eat.

African elephants have ears as big as bedspreads—the biggest ears in the world. Elephants have very good hearing, but their ears are also useful for staying cool. They can be flapped like fans, for example.

Why are zebras striped?

No one knows for sure why zebras have striped coats, but it must help them see one another so that they can stay together in a herd. There's safety in numbers, of course—especially against hungry lions!

No two zebras have exactly the same pattern of stripes—just as no two people have exactly the same fingerprints!

Some things give you spots in front of your eyes, but a herd of galloping zebras would give you stripes! For a lion, it must be even harder to pick which zebra to chase.

Why do leopards have spots?

A leopard's spots help it hide among trees and bushes so that it can pounce and surprise its prey. The light and dark patches on its fur match the patches of sunlight and shadow under the leafy branches.

Which animal changes color?

Chameleons usually have brown-green skin, but it takes them only a few minutes to change their color completely! In the sun, these strange animals turn pale to reflect bright light. When they are cold, they turn darker to absorb more of the sun's light. Chameleons also change color when they are angry or frightened.

The fur of some animals that live in cold countries is brown in the summer and white in the winter. This makes it harder for other animals to see them when snow covers the ground.

Why are flamingos pink?

Flamingos get their pink color from their favorite food—shrimp! If these leggy birds don't get enough shrimp to eat, they turn a dull gray.

Why do birds have feathers?

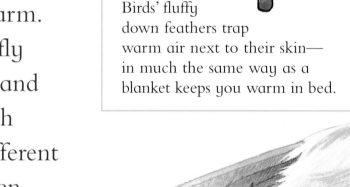

Feathers keep birds warm. They also help them fly by giving their wings and bodies a special sleek shape. Each kind of bird has feathers of a different color and pattern. Males are often brighter than females—their good looks help them attract mates!

Birds' fluffy down feathers trap warm air next to their skin— in much the same way as a blanket keeps you warm in bed.

Hummingbirds are among the world's smallest birds. The bee hummingbird lays its eggs in a nest the size of a walnut.

Which bird can fly backward?

Hummingbirds are the helicopters of the bird world. They can fly in all directions— backward, forward, sideways, up, and down. They can even hover in one spot.

Why can't penguins fly?

Penguins can't fly because their wings are too small to keep their heavy bodies up in the air. But penguins are very good swimmers and divers. They use their wings as paddles in the water.

Most birds can fold their wings up close to their bodies. But penguins can't. They always hold their wings stiffly out to the side.

Ostrich are too big to fly, but they can run at twice the speed of the fastest Olympic runners.

Which frogs can fly?

Tree frogs can climb trees, and some kinds can even glide from one tree to another! These unusual frogs have big feet with long webbed toes. When they spread their toes out, the webs of skin between them act as parachutes and help the frogs glide.

Flying fish don't really fly. Instead, they leap out of the water and then spread out extra-long fins, which help them glide. They do this to escape from their enemies.

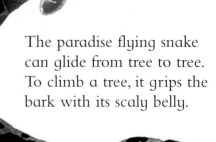

The paradise flying snake can glide from tree to tree. To climb a tree, it grips the bark with its scaly belly.

Which animals can walk upside down?

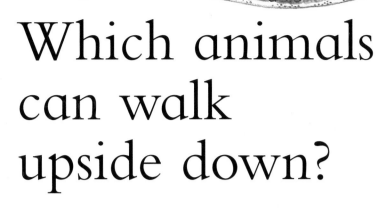

Geckos are small lizards, and some can walk upside down! They have special toes that help them cling on.

The ridges on a gecko's toes are covered in tiny bristles, each of which ends in a tiny sucker pad.

Unlike most fish, mudskippers can get oxygen from air as well as water. This allows them to stay alive out of water.

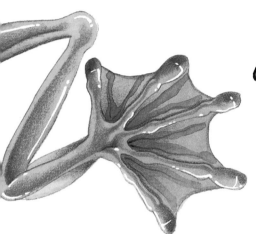

Which fish can climb trees?

The last place you'd expect to see a fish is up a tree—but, then, the mudskipper is a very odd fish! It climbs with its leglike fins, clinging on with a sort of suction cup on its belly.

How high can a kangaroo hop?

For their size, fleas are the world's best high jumpers. They can jump 100 times their own height.

Believe it or not, big kangaroos can hop right over your head! As far as we know, the highest a kangaroo has ever jumped is around 10 feet (3m)—more than twice as high as you are. Their big, strong back legs help kangaroos become such good high jumpers.

By hopping in giant leaps, big kangaroos can move almost as fast as racehorses.

How fast can a cheetah run?

Cheetahs use their sharp claws to grip and push against the ground as they race along. Olympic runners have spikes on their shoes for the same reason.

A hungry cheetah can sprint faster than 60 miles per hour (100km/h) when chasing something to eat. But running this fast soon wears it out, and it has to stop to get its breath back.

Kangaroos use their tails to balance as they hop. They'd probably fall flat on their faces if they didn't.

Which animal has an extra hand?

Some South American monkeys can grip tree branches with just their tails, leaving their hands free to pick fruit and nuts to eat. Unlike most monkeys, whose tails are completely covered with fur, they have bare skin at the ends of their tails—a lot like the palm of your hand.

Sloths are very strange, slow South American animals. They climb upside down through the treetops, and it can take them a day to move 330 feet (100m)!

How many ants can an anteater eat?

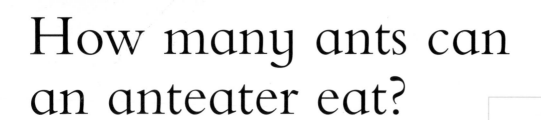

On a good day, a giant anteater eats an amazing 30,000 ants! It can scoop up as many as 500 with each flick of its long, sticky tongue. Anteaters don't munch their food because they have no teeth. They swallow the ants whole.

Giant anteaters have to walk on the knuckles of their front feet because their claws are so long and sharp. They use these claws to rip anthills apart.

Bears tear bees' nests apart to get at the honey inside. They don't seem to mind getting stung.

Birds that feed on fish often have long, sharp beaks. The anhinga uses its beak to spear fish.

Which animal uses its finger as a fork?

A strange monkeylike animal called an aye-aye has one very long, thin finger on each hand. It uses these spindly fingers to poke under tree bark for grubs and insects to eat. Then it skewers them, using its fingers a little like the way you would use a fork.

Which is the greediest animal?

For its size, the tiny Etruscan shrew has the world's biggest appetite. It hardly ever stops eating! By the time it's fully grown, it has to eat three times its own weight in food every day.

An adult Etruscan shrew weighs less than a sugar cube.

Which animals shoot their food?

If an archerfish spots an insect sitting on a plant above the water, it shoots it—not with an arrow or a bullet, of course, but with a jet of water squirted from its mouth. The insect falls into the water and the fish gobbles it up.

The bolas spider swings a thread with a sticky blob at the end to catch insects. A bola is a lasso used by South American cowboys.

The archerfish is a good shot. It can hit an insect up to 10 feet (3m) away from it.

The sound of the pistol shrimp's big left pincer snapping shut sends shock waves through the water, stunning small fish and making them easier to catch.

Which animals drink blood?

The world's most bloodthirsty animals are vampire bats, mosquitoes, and some kinds of leeches. Vampire bats don't usually drink people's blood, but mosquitoes and leeches aren't as picky!

Leeches swell up as they feed. Only some kinds suck blood.

Which birds use fish bait?

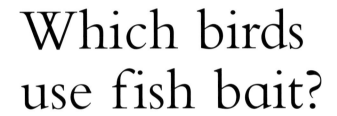

Green herons use insects and feathers as bait to catch fish. A heron drops its bait in the water and then waits for a fish to spot it. The fish thinks it has found a tasty snack but ends up as a meal for the heron instead!

Why do opossums play dead?

If the Virginia opossum is attacked, it sometimes tries to fool its enemy into leaving it alone by playing dead. Its eyes turn glassy, and it lies still, with its tongue hanging out. It's more usual—and safer—for an opossum to run away, though, or to climb a tree!

Grass snakes try to escape from their enemies by playing dead, too.

Which is the smelliest animal?

The skunk is a very smelly creature. If an enemy makes the mistake of getting too close, the skunk sprays it with a stinky oily liquid. The terrible smell can last for days.

Which is the prickliest animal?

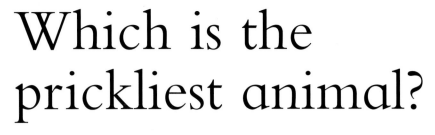

Porcupines are more prickly than any pincushion. Their backs are covered in hundreds of long, sharp quills, with barbs like fishhooks on the ends.

If a porcupine is attacked, it raises and spreads its quills, rattling them as a warning. Then it rushes backward toward its enemy.

Porcupine fish blow themselves up into prickly balls when enemies attack.

Some crabs have their own bodyguards. They carry a sea anemone in each claw so that the anemones' tentacles can sting any enemies that get too close.

Do animals kill people?

Many animals are dangerous if they are hunting for food or if something frightens them. But very few animals will attack people for no reason.

Tigers usually hunt large animals such as deer. But if a tiger is too sick to hunt, it may attack people instead.

The tiny poison-arrow frogs of South America ooze deadly poison from their brightly colored skin.

Are all snakes poisonous?

Not all snakes are poisonous. And only a few have poison strong enough to kill people. The most deadly are sea snakes, cobras, vipers, and rattlesnakes.

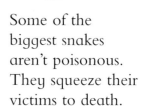

Some of the biggest snakes aren't poisonous. They squeeze their victims to death.

Are all sharks dangerous?

Many sharks are meat eaters, but very few attack people. Although millions of people swim in areas where there are sharks, there are fewer than 1,000 shark attacks a year.

The great white shark sometimes attacks swimmers.

Some of the great white shark's teeth are longer than your fingers!

Cobras have poisonous fangs.

Sharkskin is so rough that it was once used as sandpaper.

Sharks can grow a new set of teeth every two weeks.

Index